Simple Machines

By Allan Fowler

Consultant
Janann V. Jenner, Ph.D.

Children's Press®
A Division of Grolier Publishing
New York   London   Hong Kong   Sydney
Danbury, Connecticut

Visit Children's Press® on the Internet at:
http://publishing.grolier.com

Designer: Herman Adler Design Group
Photo Researcher: Caroline Anderson
The photo on the cover shows two girls using a kind of lever called a seesaw.

Library of Congress Cataloging-in-Publication Data

Fowler, Allan.
    Simple machines / by Allan Fowler.
      p. cm. — (Rookie read-about science)
    Includes index.
    Summary: Describes and compares the four kinds of simple machines—
levers, pulleys, wheels, and ramps.
    ISBN 0-516-21680-5 (lib. bdg.)   0-516-27310-8 (pbk.)
    1. Simple machines—Juvenile literature. [1. Simple machines.]
I. Title. II. Series.
TJ147.F65   2001
621.81'1—dc21
                                                     99-057025

We use machines
(muh-SHEENS) every
day. Machines help
make our lives easier.

Some machines, such as lawn mowers and vacuum (VAK-yoom) cleaners, have many parts.

Lawn mower

Vacuum cleaner

These everyday things are simple machines.

Other machines have
few parts. They are
called simple machines.

Levers, inclined planes,
wheels and axles (AK-suls),
and pulleys are four kinds
of simple machines.

This bottle opener is a kind of lever. It helps you remove the cap from a bottle.

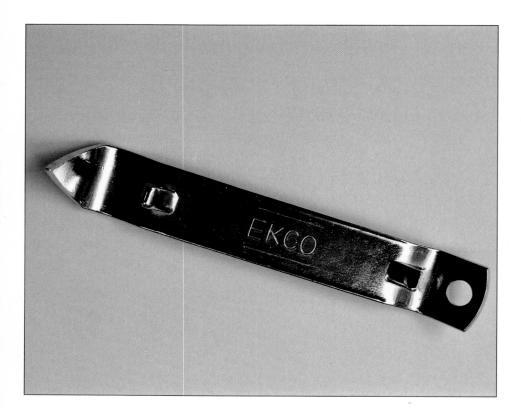

9

Some levers can help you move a heavy object, such as a rock.

Push down on one end of a lever. The other end moves up and pushes against whatever you are trying to move.

This boy is using a lever called a crowbar.

12

Have you ever ridden
a seesaw?

A seesaw is a kind of
lever. One side goes
up, while the other
side goes down.

13

Inclined planes are all
around you.

A plane is just a flat
surface, like a wooden
board. An inclined plane
is a flat surface that
is slanted.

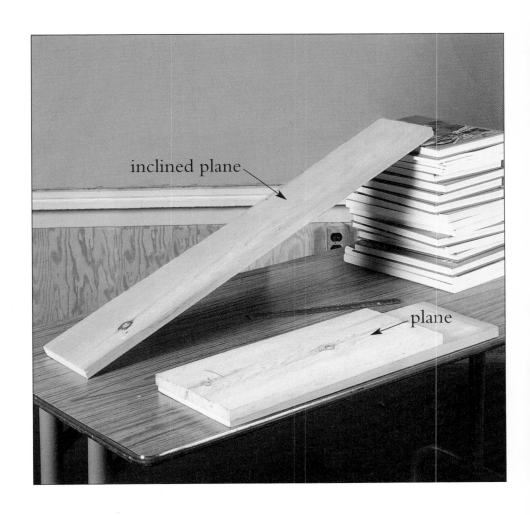

inclined plane

plane

15

Ramps are inclined planes.
It is easier to push a big load
up a ramp than to lift it.

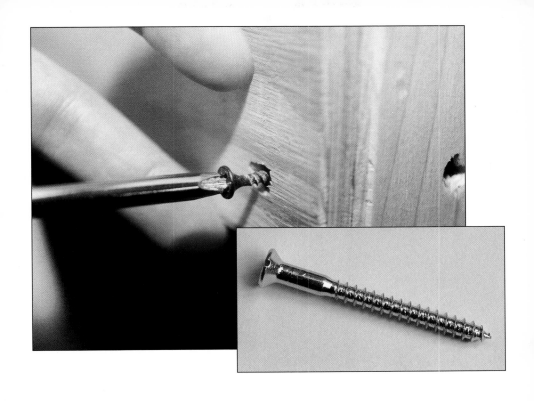

A screw is an inclined
plane wrapped around
a rod. Screws help hold
things together.

wedge

18

A wedge (wej) is another kind of inclined plane.

A wedge can help you cut wood. When a wedge is hit with a big hammer, its thin part splits the wood.

Wheels help things go.
An axle, or rod, connects
a pair of wheels. The axle
helps the wheels turn.

axle

Wheels are on bicycles
and cars.

It would be very hard
to move a bike or car
without wheels.

A pulley helps you lift heavy objects. A pulley's rope passes over a small wheel. Pull down on one end of the rope. You can lift a very heavy load tied to the other end.

pulley

pulley

A pulley can help you
raise and lower the flag
on a flagpole.

You can even lift the sail on a boat using a pulley.

These children are using two kinds of simple machines.

A wheelbarrow is a kind of lever, and it has wheels.

Have you used any simple machines today?

Words You Know

axle

inclined plane

lever

pulley

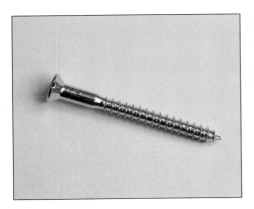

screw

seesaw

wedge

wheel

31

Index

About the Author

Allan Fowler is a freelance writer with a background in advertising.
Born in New York, he now lives in Chicago and enjoys traveling.

Photo Credits